African Moons

2004-2005 NMI
MISSION EDUCATION RESOURCES

✳ ✳ ✳

READING BOOKS

A DANGEROUS DEVOTION
Ordinary People in Extraordinary Adventures
by Carol Anne Eby

AFRICAN MOONS
by Juanita Moon

BEHIND THE VEIL
Taking Christ to Pakistanis
by Dallas Mucci

THE ROOKIE
Reflections of a New Missionary
by Tim Crutcher

TAKIN' IT TO THE STREETS
by Joe Colaizzi

WORDS OF LIFE AND LOVE
World Mission Literature Ministries
by Keith Schwanz

✳ ✳ ✳

ADULT MISSION EDUCATION RESOURCE BOOK

THE MISSION CALL
Edited by Wes Eby

African Moons

by

Juanita Moon

N P H

Nazarene Publishing House
Kansas City, Missouri

10 9 8 7 6 5 4 3 2 1

Dedication

To Bill, my inspiration, my companion,
my best friend for over 57 years,
to our children, Beverly and Mike,
and by extension to all MKs
who spend their lives adjusting.

South Africa

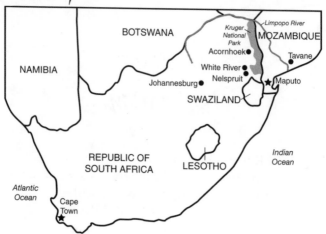

Swaziland

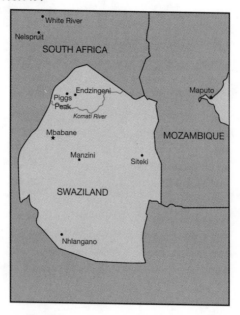

Contents

Juanita Moon and her husband, Bill, were Nazarene missionaries for 32 years (1956-88) in Africa. Juanita was a nurse; Bill, an educator. Though their original assignment was Mozambique, they were denied visas due to political unrest in the country. They were assigned to Swaziland, where they served most of their missionary career. During their last term, the Moons were once again asked to work in Mozambique; however, conditions forced them to keep their residence in Swaziland and they commuted back and forth between the neighboring nations. "This last term finally working in Mozambique," Mrs. Moon writes, "was fulfilling beyond our wildest expectations."

Mrs. Moon earned a bachelor's in nursing from the Samaritan Hospital School of Nursing, Northwest Nazarene College (now University), in 1950. While a missionary, besides nursing, she served as a health center supervisor, school evangelism coordinator, mission station hostess, and bookkeeper.

The Moons have two children, Beverly Bradley and Mike, who have given their parents four granddaughters. In retirement, Juanita and Bill reside in Colorado Springs, Colorado.

Foreword

"Missionary work is still a perilous calling," proclaimed a headline in the Colorado Springs *Gazette* on April 29, 2001. Whether in this millennium or in the last century, being a career missionary is not for wimps. The challenges of today may be different than those of yesterday, but when it comes to missionary service, cowards need not apply.

This book provides a picture of missionary lives in the in-between years—between the intrepid pioneers who blazed the way for their replacements and today's courageous champions of the gospel who continue to open mission frontiers around the globe. This story is an important one, for it helps us better understand missions in the 21st century.

Juanita Moon has chronicled a part of her and Bill's lives as missionaries for 32 years in Africa. Writing about hardships and heartaches, valleys and victories, problems and praises, Juanita has captured the essence of missionary life viewed through the lens of a woman, wife, mother, and nurse. Her skill with words leaves the reader chuckling one moment and crying the next. Clearly, the Moons were not wimps.

"I want to be realistic about the challenges and difficulties that missionaries face," Juanita writes; "however, the joys and rewards are numerous and real. It is an adventure with Christ, and Bill and I had fun. Whatever else missions is, it's certainly not boring."

Juanita certainly conveys in this story that missions was an adventure for her family. No humdrum existence at all for the Moon tribe.

I commend this book to you. Read it, but read with care. God just may call you to Swaziland . . . or Samoa . . . or Spain . . . or Sri Lanka . . . or . . .

Nina G. Gunter
General NMI Director

Fleas and Fish Wives

"Are you at this very moment clearly in the experience of entire sanctification?" The strong, gravely voice came from General Superintendent D. I. Vanderpool. As I looked around the room into the five somber faces, I thought I had suddenly been ushered into the judgment room of God. After my husband, Bill, and I caught our breath, we humbly answered, "Yes."

"You understand, don't you, that we aren't sending you on an extended tourist trip," another general superintendent stated.

"Are your children completely on the altar?" came the question from another direction.

Visions appeared before me of our two beautiful children, Beverly, age four, and Mike, not yet two. This last question pushed the wrong button; tears burst from my eyes. Who says a woman's tears aren't useful? The mood changed and the five general superintendents showed us their true side of being caring and compassionate.

This overwhelming interview was the culmination of our months and years of attempts to fulfill

God's call and our heart's desire to serve Him in missions. Assurance came with the promise, "My Presence will go with you" (Exod. 33:14, NIV).

We returned home to Friend, Nebraska, where Bill was teaching in the high school. We had no idea what the outcome of our interviews would be. Then one day came the phone call, "Congratulations, you are appointed to Mozambique."

I was silent.

"Is there a problem?" the secretary asked. "Didn't you want to go there?"

"Oh . . . no problem. . . ." I stammered. "I just haven't a clue where it is."

"It's a Portuguese province in southeastern Africa. First you must go to Portugal to learn the language. We have no Nazarenes there, but you will

Moons leaving for Africa, 1956

find a Dr. Cecil Scott who will act as a liaison for you."

✽ ✽ ✽

Lisbon, October 10, 1956. Phyllis Scott was up, drinking her usual early morning tea by a window that overlooked Portugal's historic Tagus estuary. She saw the beautiful ocean liner *Independence* entering the harbor. She dashed to awaken her husband who was trying to nurse a cold. "My dear, I do believe the Moons are arriving."

Cecil Scott hurriedly searched for our pictures and went to the docks to meet us.

After bringing us back to the *Liga* (Evangelical League) and serving us the customary cup of tea, Dr. Scott took us in his quaint little British car to a *pensão* (boardinghouse). He assured us that someone there spoke English. Whoever that someone was must have been on vacation. We never saw him or her.

In our room we surveyed the surroundings— one double bed and two singles cots. In the corner was a lovely antique water pitcher and wash basin, a bidet, and a bucket. A single lightbulb glowed in the ceiling without reaching the corners of the room. We had arrived. We were missionaries at last!

Near noon Bill went looking for a dining room. With a little sleuthing he reported that lunch would begin at 1:30. At the proper time we were formally seated at a table covered with a starched white cloth. At each place setting was a stack of four plates and a soup bowl, plus an array of unfamiliar silverware. The waiter served us a savory soup. Then he

13

removed the bowl, uncovering the plate for the next course—fish. The whole sea creature complete with big eyes stared accusingly at us. Bev took one look and asked if it was dead yet.

How happy we were to find the last course was luscious, familiar fruit. The other diners smiled as we ate the fruit with our hands. Everyone else used proper eating utensils. While we never managed to acquire the skill of eating an orange with a knife and fork, eventually we learned to dissect a banana properly.

That night I was awakened with a terrible itching on my feet and legs. The morning light revealed great welts. As I stared at my mottled lower limbs, I thought I saw something jump.

Dominating the living area was a huge, generously flyspecked, Italian crystal chandelier.

Soon the Scotts arrived with two American ladies who were also studying language. They graciously offered to take the children to the park while Dr. and Mrs. Scott helped us look for an apartment. One of the women was a medical doctor, and I tried discreetly to tell her that I must have contracted something horrible. She smiled and rubbed her chin. "I believe you have fleas."

Fleas! My first day and I have fleas! "What *do* I do?"

"Just learn to live with them," was her practical reply.

The Scotts had an apartment picked out for us.

14

They assured us that we were "jolly fortunate" to find such a nicely furnished place. It was classified as modern because it boasted a four-foot "fridge." The apartment was typical of the city, a grand mixture of culture and taste. Everything was for show; nothing, practical. Dominating the living area was a huge, generously flyspecked, Italian crystal chandelier. The children's mattresses were dusty straw. Ours was hard and lumpy with kapok.

One night I awoke to find Bill beating on the pillow. "What in the world are you doing?" I queried.

"Just trying to make a place for my ear."

Bill and I counted 80 antique pictures, platters, and plates adorning the walls. We had a two-year-old boy who liked to throw things. However, it was to be just a few months. Right?

Mrs. Scott graciously took me shopping for food, and the first stop was the grocery. I did not recognize one item. Behind an overloaded counter, a smiling gentleman stood waiting for my bidding. I looked for Crisco. I saw a tub of lard and one of butter each with a paddle protruding. How many grams did I want? *What are grams?* I wondered. On request the helpful clerk put a piece of paper on the scale and measured out a quantity, folded the paper adeptly, and put it in my shopping basket. Sugar and flour were in fragile paper bags; eggs were in a basin in the hot, sunny window. Baking soda was scooped from a container, weighed on the scale, and enfolded in a scrap of paper. All items were placed in a shopping basket to be carried by a delivery boy to our back door. A lady would never walk on the street carrying a parcel. I wondered if the cake would be mixed before I arrived home.

The butchery, identified by a cascade of hanging strings of beads designed to discourage flies, was just a few doors down the street. Whole sides of beef hung in the open. Carcases of smaller animals exposed their skinless selves, unembarrassed. The shopper named the muscle wanted and again the number of grams. I tried to remember the page from *Joy of Cooking* that indicated the way to cut up a side of beef. But the names of the muscles? And in a foreign language? Where were those tidy little packages with labels on them to tell me whether to fry, bake, or broil?

I bargained for vegetables and fruit from vendors on the street. Some sellers had a donkey pulling a handsomely decorated cart, loaded with goods. The women carried their merchandise on their heads. Prices were negotiable.

I'd always heard the phrase "screaming like a fish wife," but this was the first time to hear it for real. The women brought the early morning catch through the streets and with shrill, strident calls advertised their wares piled in flat wicker baskets on their heads. Since I am taller than most Portuguese women, those baskets passed just under my nose. Once when I brought home a purchase from a fishwife, "it" showed signs of life, so the kids put "it" in a pan of water. It began swimming around. That is what is called fresh!

Bread—wonderful, crusty, warm rolls—were delivered at our door every morning. We ate lots of it, along with real butter.

Fishermen drawing in their nets from the sea

❋ ❋ ❋

I couldn't imagine the luxury of a maid, but it was soon evident that a local person could earn her meager wage by doing the marketing for our family. She was much more familiar with what the prices should be and not inflated because the customer was an American. But we faced a small problem: our first maid had never worked for a foreigner before, knew not one word of English, and did not know how to cook anything besides boiled, salted cod fish. Yet she was pleasant, eager to learn, and fond of the children. And a Christian. A maid's room gave us a live-in baby-sitter.

Laundry was done on the built-in concrete scrub board in a concrete tub on the back step. Lines, strung alongside the building complex, operated with a pulley. I was pleased to see the first laundered clothes hanging outside. Bev's white socks were snow-white; the stains were gone but so were the soles. That scrub board along with generous amounts of strong bleach had done the trick.

Living in Lisbon was a great adventure. The city, picturesque and historic, melded the past and present together. Flowers adorned and filled every open space. Hanging flower baskets graced windowsills and lampposts.

Our family visited different evangelical churches. The evening services began at 9:30. One evening Bill felt impressed to attend a certain church. During the introductions the word *Nazareno* captured Bill's attention; this he understood. With the help of the pastor with limited English, he learned that a Cape Verdian Nazarene pastor, Alvaro Andrade, was in Lisbon for medical treatment.

We invited Alvaro to our house for a meal, and eventually he made our apartment his home while he suffered much at the hands of many doctors. Through him we found that Lisbon had several Nazarenes, mostly Cape Verdians who had moved to Portugal's capital for various reasons. Senhor Andrade was just the one to seek them out. With the added attraction of Cape Verdian missionaries visiting the city, we began discreet prayer meetings and fellowship times. Having more than 15 people together in a home without a police permit was illegal.

The neighbors in the same apartment building discussed what was going on in our home. We had opportunity to speak to one curious young man who demonstrated a lively interest. After some time for

18

conversation, Bill asked him, "Have you ever asked forgiveness for your sins?"

"Yes, every night," answered the young man.

"Do you know if they have been forgiven?"

"No."

"Would you like to know?"

"Yes, of course; anyone would."

"It *is* possible. Would you care to have peace in your heart before you go home tonight?"

"I would."

We invited the young man to come into the front room and pray. Bill awakened Senhor Andrade to come and help us. As it was 1:30 in the morning, we had to rouse him out of bed. We had never prayed in Portuguese before, and this was no time to practice our language skills. We all knelt and soon an "altar service" was in progress. God gloriously forgave the man's sins. This young fellow, who had never been in a Nazarene church, rejoiced over his salvation as though he had been attending camp meeting all his life and knew exactly how Nazarenes act when they get blessed.

Alvaro Andrade won our hearts. His physical welfare gave us great concern, especially when we learned the medics wanted to do exploratory brain surgery to find the cause of his

One day I cleared out the bathroom cupboard and counted 12 toothbrushes and one partial plate that no one in our family claimed.

19

headaches. With the help of a local pastor and trans-lator, we informed the physicians that this was an important gentleman and that he had many friends interested in his well-being. The surgery was can-celed. Senhor Andrade asked Bill to anoint him for healing. Pastor Alvaro recovered and returned to Cape Verde to serve 30 more years as a pastor.

✳ ✳ ✳

It was a real blessing to have the many visitors that came to our home. One day I cleared out the bathroom cupboard and counted 12 toothbrushes and one partial plate that no one in our family claimed.

No language school as such existed. Just living in Lisbon had its own learning experiences. Eventu-ally we had a working knowledge of the language and passed the required government exams. Then we were able to apply for Mozambique residence visas. In spite of the official policy of religious free-dom in Portugal and in all of its overseas provinces, government officials seemingly did not want the in-digenous people to be educated for fear they would rise to the level they could demand independence. Thus Bill, an educator, was not desired or needed. Several approaches were tried.

While waiting for the many visa requests to be processed, I studied for and passed the Portuguese nursing exams. Bill attended classes at the university.

"One day someone will look at the files in Kan-sas City," Bill suggested, "and see our names there and exclaim, 'Are they still on salary?' Then they'll

**The freighter *Moçamedes* that took the Moons
to Africa in 1956**

decide that something should be done with us."

Finally, we received word to proceed to Africa. We booked passage on the freighter *Moçamedes*. Mission authorities had hope that a residence application made from South Africa would succeed. If not, we might try going in and out of Mozambique on a renewable tourist visa for 60 days.

We eagerly began our sea voyage, following in the wake of the early explorer Vasco da Gama, to Mozambique—the place where we were certain we were going to spend the rest of our missionary career—to enjoy thousands of African moons.

Site near Lisbon from where Vasco da Gama
sailed to begin his world travels

Tavane and Tick Bites

After 40 days and 40 nights on the rolling seas, we arrived in Lourenço Marques (now Maputo), clutching our eight-day visas for Mozambique. We were met at the dock by Nazarene missionaries—the Armand Dolls and the Floyd Perkins—and Manuel Dias, a Portuguese pastor. Finally we were in Africa. We were ecstatic!

Officials in Lourenço Marques along with everyone else were sure we'd get our visas extended to 30 days. So the next day we traveled up country in Armand Doll's big four-wheel-drive vehicle to the Tavane mission station, the center for all of the Nazarene work in the country. The road—a narrow, tarred, one-lane road—started the journey. Then it changed to two tarred strips, one for each wheel. If we met another vehicle, we shared one strip. It was all a great adventure for us.

We crossed Kipling's "great, grey-green, greasy Limpopo" on a *ponte*, a ferry with Africans pulling the cables attached to the opposite riverbank, rhythmically stomping and chanting and making up songs about the passengers. Rev. Doll instructed us on the proper procedure to escape from a vehicle that just might go over the plank at the end of the ferry and dump us into the river. Most reassuring indeed! Across the Limpopo, the road abruptly changed to sand and then progressively to deep sand or mud.

New missionaries in Mozambique were rare; therefore, a tremendous surprise welcome was planned for us. We made a couple of stops at churches along the way and were greeted with crowds yelling, "Hoyo hoyo."

Close to the mission we had to cross the Mausse Plain, the bed of a sometimes-lake. The tracks were filled with water and looked formidable, but with a four-wheel-drive vehicle and its skilled driver Armand Doll, we weren't concerned. The kids laughed as we bounced off our seats, enduring bruise-making bumps. But we kept going until we took the wrong track and wound up in mud to the axles. Everyone got out and offered advice. "Jack up this wheel. Or that one." Mike got the prize when he looked out over the puddle of water and proclaimed, "Why don't you just pull up the anchor?"

Darkness came. Finally we were unstuck and on our way. Close to the station we found people still waiting, waving palm branches and shouting, "Hoyo hoyo." Church bells rang, announcing the welcome service inside. By candles and lamplight we saw hundreds of black faces with wide smiles. Actually we mostly saw white teeth flash as they picked up the reflections of the flickering kerosene lamps. Speeches were made. Gifts were given—a Shangaan Bible, a songbook, and a locally made basket to carry the two

Road to Tavane

books. A reception line followed where we learned the proper way to shake hands and then practiced it with each and everyone there. This big welcome explained Armand Doll's anxiety about getting to the mission by a certain time.

Our hearts yearned to be able to stay there. The small core of missionaries was grossly overloaded with responsibilities: a Bible college, several districts, a day school, and a clinic—the latter actually more like a small hospital with two buildings, one for maternity patients, the other for seeing and treating patients. Close by were several *rondavels*—huts for patients who needed to stay several days. No resident doctor was available.

Even daily living was a chore—two-hour trips to the post office . . . no phones . . . electricity for lights relied on the whim of a generator that would not support any appliances . . . water, quite scarce, always had to be boiled and filtered . . . hand-laundered clothes hung outside.

"Why must everything be ironed?" I asked our hostess.

"There's an insect that lays eggs on the clothing and burrows into one's skin, producing interesting larvae. Ironing kills the eggs." This was done with one of those antique charcoal irons.

We had eight days of euphoria. Bessie Grose's garage was loaded with parcels sent from Nazarene churches in the States during the past two years. We had a wonderful time opening each box with care and noting the contents along with the name of the sender. Our desire was to acknowledge each one in great detail.

Since we had not received any parcels in Lisbon and had also suffered the loss of laundry, stolen from the picturesque clothesline that ran alongside of the building, most of our clothing needed replacement. Bill's white shirt collars had been scrubbed too often on the rough slab and subjected to a copious amount of bleach. Most of the collars had been turned to hide the frayed edges.

About 4:00 P.M. on the eighth day, a runner came from the nearest telegraph post 20 miles away, stating we were to be out of the country that very day; our extensions had been denied. All care for the packages was forgotten as we just dumped all our old clothes and started picking out brand-new articles from the boxes with little regard as to who the sender was. Our hearts were sore. In spite of all the inconveniences, we felt we could help lift the other missionaries' loads and truly wanted to stay.

Tick–bite fever was most likely, and Bill was already feeling the effect of the onset of disease.

Our trip out of Mozambique was another saga. Since it was already late afternoon when we received the message, sleep was out of the question. We'd have to get up at midnight so we could be at an immigration office when it opened in the morning.

Our instructions were to go to Johannesburg. Since the field director, William Esselstyn, was out of the country, someone would meet us there. But we didn't know who.

Bill had picked up a tick while hauling stones for a building project for Mary Cooper. Tick-bite fever was most likely, and Bill was already feeling the effect of the onset of disease. As the train pulled out of the station, Bessie Grose called through our train compartment window, "I think you must get off at Germiston!"

"Where in the world is Germiston?" Bill said. "Dr. Esselstyn said, 'Go to Johannesburg.'"

We had not slept for 36 hours, so the train's compartments and beds were a marvelous sight. We all promptly collapsed in them. By this time Bill's temperature had soared, making it difficult for him to relax. But the rest of us, totally exhausted, sank into a deep sleep.

Suddenly there was a terrific banging on our compartment door. Opening it, we found Afrikaans officials being most officious and speaking English. (Our first mistake was to say we didn't understand Afrikaans.)

"Where are you going?" one asked gruffly.

"Johannesburg."

"What will be your address?"

"We don't know."

"Who is meeting you?"

"We don't know."

"How long do you plan to stay?"

"Don't know."

"How much money do you have?"

"Very little."

"What are you importing?"

"A small amount of personal goods, a typewriter, and a wind-up record player."

"Is it a gramophone or phonograph?"

"We don't know. It's there on the shelf. You may look at it!"

"Who do you know there?"

We knew Dr. Esselstyn was out of the country, and in our sleepy state we tried to remember the name of some missionary living in South Africa. We were blank. Finally we mentioned the name of "Uncle Jenkins" (Charles Jenkins). Amazingly, all was well.

We tumbled back into bed and quickly returned to needed slumber. In the morning we felt greatly improved and in better spirits. Bill's fever, however, was cyclic.

At one place we stopped longer than usual, and Bill could see the name on the platform—Germiston. Wasn't that the place where we were to get off? We went out in the corridor and looked down the platform.

We spotted a little woman with her hair in a bun. She saw us and hollered, "Moons? You are to get off here. Throw us your luggage out the window. And hurry!"

All of the missionaries were there to look us over and to guess how long we would last.

We started with what was handy, and out went Bill's briefcase with all our important papers. The train pulled out. "See you in Joni [Johannesburg]?" we heard someone call. That was our introduction to our wonderful hosts the Stockwells.

Before long we arrived in Johannesburg where we found Norman and Carol Zurcher waiting for us. They were recent arrivals on the field and had responded to a phone call to meet us. Oscar and Marge Stockwell soon arrived and took us to their home.

The next day was the official welcome for the two new missionary couples, the Moons and the Zurchers. All of the missionaries, living on the Rand (the Johannesburg area) were there to look us over and to guess how long we would last. The Zurchers, young and charming, sang together beautifully. By this time Bill's fever was raging again. He came out of the bedroom and smiled for a while. Then he sneaked back to bed and shivered until he shook the bedposts. It seemed that treatment for tick bites was a bit new. Most seemed to think a person could tough it out and never be bothered again. However, Dr. Esselstyn upon his return declared this was nonsense and quickly acquired a specific antibiotic that proved effective.

The Executive Mission Council remained optimistic that somehow we would be allowed to work in Mozambique, as the missionaries there were stretched to the limit. For many African moons we waited, living in a minute apartment close to veteran missionaries, Charles and Pearl Jenkins, and studied Shangaan, a tribal language. What a blessing this proved to be! We learned much more than language. They delighted us with stories of their adventures, how God had been faithful. We had a long discussion about demon possession. In my sheltered thinking I had assumed that the accounts of demon possession in the Bible were explained by mental illness or epilepsy. Finally Uncle Jenkins said, "Juanita, don't worry about it. When you see it, you won't need a label."

✳ ✳ ✳

Since we were still in South Africa, we explored a new tactic. We were tired of waiting. We would go into Mozambique with 60-day tourist visas as we had done in Portugal. We could not practice our "professions," but we could do much to lift the load. Miss Cooper moved into a grass hut and let us live in her house at Tavane.

Unfortunately this strategy had problems. Again we had to quickly leave. *But where should we go?* we wondered. No phone lines were available to the regional office. We were on our own.

The closest mission station in South Africa was just on the other side of Kruger National Park in the northeastern corner of South Africa. Leaving Mozambique in a hurry, we spent one night in this beautiful game reserve, and then we proceeded on to Acornhoek where the church had a hospital. Our good friends from former days, John and Lucille Sutherland were stationed there, but they had no idea we were coming. Darkness fell. The roads were strange. There were no lights or sign of human habitation, only animal sounds in the darkness. We were without food and water. The kids were tired. We were emotionally and physically exhausted.

We drove on to the mission hospital grounds, and someone directed us to the Sutherland home. Dr. John opened the door to see this ragged-looking family and said, "Oh! Oh, I'll get John Mark out of the tub immediately."

Here we discovered that the missionaries had already received word that, if something happened and the Moons had to leave Mozambique, we were to go to Acornhoek and help prepare for the upcoming meeting of the All-African Nazarene Mission Council. God had been faithful to guide us. That was exactly what we had done.

At this council meeting, we were assigned to Endzingeni, Swaziland.

3

Storms and Simplicity Patterns

After four years of living out of suitcases and having no "fixed abode" and no more than a tourist visa for any country for more than 60 days, we were anxious to be settled—well, at least for a little while. We smiled as we recalled the remark at our interview with the general superintendents, "We are not sending you out on an extended tourist trip."

We were assigned to work in northern Swaziland at the mother station, Endzingeni, the launching place for all of the work in Africa. Endzingeni, a beautiful mountain station where Harmon Schmelzenbach and two of his children are buried, is about 12 miles from Piggs Peak.

Bill's assignment was to teach in the high school and be the *grantee* of the 20 Nazarene schools on the zone. What is a grantee? Just the liaison between the mission and the government. What an understatement that was!

Schools had a long history in Swaziland that began with the Schmelzenbachs teaching preacher candidates to read. These preachers, in turn, would go to an outpost and establish a church and teach during the week. Thus schools were established at most of the places where there was a church.

As development proceeded, qualified teachers were provided by our own teacher's college. Eventually the government assumed the salaries of the teachers. Still, all was under the authority of the Church of the Nazarene. Bill, as grantee, was the liaison between the teacher, church, and government.

We lived in what we affectionately called the "mud house." Once a stable, it had been remodeled for a mission home. The walls had barely enough paint on them to hold the mud plaster. If the paint skin broke, a great pile of red soil suddenly appeared

The "mud house" at Endzingeni

from a gaping hole. A straight line could not be found anywhere in the house. I wanted to hang the drapes that I had used in our previous apartment. They would fit the large picture window and give us privacy. However, should the top line be straight, or should I hem the bottoms to be even?

Nevertheless it was a house where we could open our belongings. Most had been packed for four years. Beverly buried her face in a faded tablecloth and said. "Look, Mom, this is ours." Some things had to be discarded.

At Endzingeni I home-schooled Mike. This is a little insight into his study and personality. At the end of a series of lessons on hygiene were some questions. One asked: How can you keep clean? After a very long time of contemplation, Mike responded, "Stay in bed all day and not play."

✳   ✳   ✳

As each lightning bolt struck and lit up the sky, they danced and shouted in a challenging competition to the thunder.

Living in Colorado I thought I had experienced thunderstorms, but they were nothing compared to the ones we had in Swaziland. Perhaps it was the quantity of iron in the soil that attracts lightning. Whatever it was, it was awesome. The buildings had roofs of corrugated iron that amplified the impact of hail that rattled in an accompaniment to the rolling thunder.

One day Mike and Nebbie, daughter of missionary colleagues, Herman and Mary Spencer, were playing at our house when a big thunderstorm hit. I was teaching at the high school and sprinted home to comfort those poor, scared kids—or so I thought. No frightened children there! They were bursting with joy and excitement. As each lightning bolt struck and lit up the sky, they danced and shouted in a challenging competition to the thunder.

Beverly went with the two Spencer girls to a weekday boarding school at Piggs Peak. This meant they went on Monday and came home Friday.

Our daughter had to have a uniform. I asked the school headmaster where we obtained these. He suggested that the material was available at a local store at Piggs Peak. The pattern? He kindly took out an envelope and sketched. It was just a simple dress, dropped waistline, buttoned-down front, capped sleeves, white Peter Pan collar, and cuffs. No problem. Fortunately I had enough Simplicity patterns that I could put it together. "And what about the 'jerseys' or sweaters?" I asked.

"Oh, the mothers just knit them." I learned to knit!

A new assignment fell in our laps: keeping financial books. All students paid school fees, hostel fees, domestic science fees, and so forth. Next problem: money in Swaziland was tied to the South African coin, which was based on the British system. Everything was in pounds, shillings, and pence. (Just for review, there were 12 pence in a shilling and 20 shillings in a pound. Add the pence to 20, carry one,

Endzingeni mission station

add the shillings to 12, carry one.) We had no adding machine. Many an African moon shone as tears were shed over balancing those books.

Piggs Peak and Patients

After our first furlough in the shadow of Pikes Peak in Colorado, we were delighted to be assigned to Piggs Peak, a village named for Mr. Pigg, who had discovered gold in the area. Bill would be the head of station, which meant a general caretaker. Also, he was grantee for the 20 Nazarene schools in the northern zone.

I would be the sister-in-charge of the health center. Juanita Gardner, who had been a super efficient and much-loved supervisor, was transferring to Endzingeni.

Three problems waited for a man to be the head of station: (1) light plant—"bruck," (2) wiring—lightning struck, (3) water—muck.

Let me offer a bit of explanation. (1) The light plant was powered by a little diesel engine that supplied lights for our house and the clinic. It also ran the little diesel pump for water storage. But it was broken, or "bruck" as some Southerners might say. (2) The wiring had been done in the early '40s by Paul Schmelzenbach, son of the pioneer missionary Harmon Schmelzenbach, when he should have been

37

preaching. It was far from code. A few months before our arrival, lightning struck the area and every plug-in and light fixture in the house popped off the wall.

(3) In the '20s when the mission was first established at Piggs Peak, a ditch was dug that diverted water from a nearby stream into a little rivulet that ran through the mission, behind the dispensary, and past our back door. It served its purpose for many years as a convenient water supply. A small diesel pump forced the water into a storage tank placed on a platform at the clinic and then into pipes that supplied the clinic and our house. The water then had to be filtered and boiled. It was OK for bathing—if not too muddy, that is. I overheard Beverly instruct-

Juanita and Bill Moon at Piggs Peak, 1967

ing Mike, "If you slip in from the back of the tub slowly you won't disturb the mud that has settled in the front."

Besides our family, about 40 other residents were on the mission compound: teachers, various helpers, nurses, aids, and clinic patients, as well as 350 school children. And no clean water.

Our children were delighted to be able to attend the English-speaking (European) school at Piggs Peak and stay at home.

Beverly went into standard V (grade seven). This was the first time she had started and finished a year in the same school. She adapted well, considering all the changes. Beverly enjoyed all the babies and toddlers that needed and responded to her TLC. They were delightful, cherubic tykes who loved her. The domestic science teacher had a newborn that Beverly adopted as her own real live "doll" by taking over much of her care, including her baths.

Mike became fast friends with the pastor's sons with whom he shared a number of adventures, some of which we were blissfully ignorant until many years later.

The present clinic was built in the '30s. It replaced the original Raleigh Fitkin Hospital that was moved to Manzini. The buildings of the former hospital are used as classrooms. The clinic was a U-shaped building. One leg of the U housed the resident nurse, a workroom, and the delivery room. The base of the U was a long ward with beds for mothers with their newborn babies snuggled in wooden box-beds by their side. The medicine room was next where many of the drugs were mixed and bottled according to a little black "recipe" book. Adjacent was the examining room next to a small office. The other leg of the U had several rooms opening off a veranda where inpatients could remain for a few days when necessary. A storage room at the end completed the U.

I suddenly realized I needed to practice what I learned in first aid. I slipped to my office, put my head between my knees, and prayed.

Delivering babies was another challenge. Electricity depended on the little diesel engine to run the generator that was only used for lights and only for a few hours each night. There was no running water, no autoclave for sterilizing, no sterile gowns, no drapes, and no gloves. Instruments were boiled with the aid of covered steel bowls and a primus stove. With no specialized training in midwifery, I asked the well-trained Swazi nurse-midwife, "Tell me when you have a delivery so I can observe the procedure." While I was observing the successful delivery of the first baby, I suddenly realized I needed to practice what I learned in first aid. I slipped to my office, put my head between my knees, and prayed. I couldn't imagine how I could possibly cope with all that was expected of me.

The clinics or health centers in those days were the cutting edge of the ministry of the church. They reached people who had no contact with the church.

Juanita Moon teaching a health lesson outside a clinic

Over the years they had developed a reputation of quality care with a spiritual influence.

From our hospital in Manzini, the best source of medical help in all of Swaziland, one missionary doctor would make a routine visit to each clinic once a month. These kind and experienced doctors were our mentors as they gave us standing orders and answered our long list of questions at each visit.

The early morning walk from our home along a protective corridor of pine trees always lifted my spirits. As I gazed out over the mountains that stretched into the distance, I truly lifted my eyes unto the hills and to the Creator of this fabulously beautiful corner of creation and asked for wisdom and strength for the day. Already I could see knots of patients gathering around the clinic. Most had

41

walked for miles. The fortunate found the required fare to ride a Swazi taxi (bus). I smiled that I did not have to earn the confidence of the community. It had been earned by my predecessors dating from the '20s and more recently by Juanita Gardner. Although she tried, she could not transfer to me all the wisdom that she had gained.

What will greet me today? I wondered, as I strolled into the clinic. An epidemic of whooping cough seemed to be in abeyance. The usual childhood inoculations were available but were not universal, though the fee was nominal. I dreaded the spread of measles. For an undernourished child, complications were common and serious.

This first patient that day was a toddler. Putting him on my lap, I could diagnose the problem without the help of any lab. When I tried to look at his throat with the aid of a tongue depressor, I was confronted with clenched teeth and a spirit of absolute defiance. After questioning the mother my diagnosis was confirmed. The child had a sore throat and had suffered an attempt by his mother to "wash" the back of the throat by scraping away the white or yellow spots with a fingernail she kept long for just such a purpose. The tyke now had a full-blown infection with a high fever.

Kwashiorkor! I couldn't even pronounce the word a year ago, much less try to spell it. Kwashiorkor is the name for the disease of a child who has been bumped off the breast by a younger baby. The "bumped" child is fed only white cornmeal, which an infant can't digest, often put in a bottle with wa-

Bill Moon holding a child ill with kwashiorkor

ter to make it look like milk. The symptoms are severe protein deficiency characterized by edema in the limbs and reddish, straight hair. We found a cheap food concentrate, Pro Nutro, that was something like Pablum but had a heavy concentration of processed protein. This product saved many lives.

I learned about *bilharzia* and more than I wanted to know concerning other parasites, which were common. Someone has said that if God has a sense of humor He must have laughed His socks off when He created the variety of parasites found in Africa.

Typhoid could be spotted across the room. The victim's eyes were sunken and held an anxious expression. This disease was accompanied by fever, diarrhea, and a distinctive odor. A lab report, if I could get one, took at least two weeks. By then the patient could be dead.

On regular days in the clinic we handled many usual problems, but some of them were complicated because of previous treatment with traditional medicine. Common lore was that a disease had to be cleansed from the body. This was done by giving a potion that caused both vomiting and/or diarrhea. I learned that I should not query a mother if she had given an enema. Instead, I asked, "How many enemas have you given today?" Often the diarrhea could not be stopped, and the child quickly became dehydrated.

On examination we often saw *elevenses*. This indicated that the patients had been to the witch doctor, who had made two parallel cuts, usually with a

Patients waiting at the Piggs Peak clinic

44

razor blade, that looked like *1*1s over the afflicted area so that the spirit causing the disease could exit. In reflecting upon this practice, I sometimes wonder if this activity, along with other traditional treatments using unsterilized instruments, contributed to the wide spread of AIDS.

When an epidemic of smallpox hit Swaziland, my first patient was Sibusiso, the child of a nurse's aide. The boy experienced convulsions but had no other obvious symptoms. Although I was in the middle of preparing a birthday dinner for Bill, the Swazi nurse and I took the child to the hospital at Manzini. There he developed the typical blisters. After the doctor diagnosed the illness, he sent the child back to the clinic—with *me*.

"I don't have any idea about the nursing care for smallpox," I said to my staff nurse. "All I know are the little scratches you make for vaccination."

"What would you do if you had a patient in America with smallpox?" she countered.

"Panic!" I was right on schedule.

Other local customs had to be dealt with. For example, the custom of putting cow dung on a baby's fontanel to cause it to close didn't do much harm; however, if the baby was born at home and the dung was applied to the cord, we had big problems—tetanus.

It was known that if a patient was too sick to be treated at our clinic we could be persuaded to transport the patient to our hospital at Manzini, which was 60-plus miles and two hours away. This resulted in many interesting trips on mostly dirt roads.

45

Komati River at flood stage

The journey to Manzini necessitated crossing the Komati River that carved its way through the mountains. We had two choices. The closest way, known as the "upper" road, went through the town of Mbabane. This route crossed the Komati with a low-level, one-way bridge spanning a narrow, deep gorge. When there was lots of rain, the river flooded, making it impossible to cross. This forced us to take the longer route, or the "lower" road. It also had a low, one-way bridge, but the water-carrying capacity was greater. Even so, it often flooded too.

One day one of our female teachers and her husband came to the clinic. She had been in labor for over 24 hours. Finding transportation to the Peak from her home, 10 miles out in the country, had been difficult. Earlier, on her required examination by a doctor, he told her that if she had a small baby she could probably deliver the child. If not, she would have to travel to the hospital at Manzini for delivery. Right away it was obvious to me this was going to be a difficult birth.

I started to Manzini with the woman in labor in the back seat of our car. The seasonal rains, which had already begun, were coming down with great force. I heard that the "upper" road was already flooded; we'd have to take the "lower" route. As we passed Endzingeni and started down the hill, kids along the road were waving and gesturing, but we didn't know why. When we sighted the river, we could see why. Large trees were tumbling and swirling along in a great rush over the bridge. What to do? We had no choice. We returned to Piggs Peak.

Surprise! We had visitors. Some missionaries from Manzini had gone to a funeral in South Africa and were returning via Piggs Peak. They couldn't cross the river either, so they had to stay with us until the river went down.

Among the visitors was David Hynd, a medical doctor. With his order of medication that we would not dare use on our own, a successful delivery was accomplished. We praised the Lord for His timing and care.

At one of the large Nazarene outstations, Helehele, the community had requested a clinic for years. Located on a craggy mountaintop, Helehele had a well-established church and large school. Juanita Gardner had traveled there periodically and treated patients on a bench under a tree, close to the turnoff that began the ascent to the school. Now I would resume the occasional visits. The community people offered us a mud and wattle room at a store close to the school.

The only available vehicle was our family car, not a four-wheel drive. Bill planned to take me the first time, along with Juanita Gardner, who had started the contact. Esther Thomas, the nurse at Endzingeni, wanted to visit Helehele as well, since she had never been there. When the two nurses arrived at the Peak, they found a teacher at our back door and a school committee at the front door, all waiting to see Bill. The ladies suggested we smuggle Bill out through the bathroom window. After the current emergencies were solved we were on our way.

Juanita, Esther, and I sat on a log and looked out over a series of beautiful, hazy valleys and mountains that stretched into the mysterious uncharted distance.

While waiting for us, Bill used the time to visit the school's building project. With about 400 children enrolled, four classes met in the church building. The school inspector had once compared it to a market where every teacher was crying his wares. Bill was surprised to learn that the drums had been beating. The local people, reasoning that he would be the chauffeur for this difficult drive, had four committees awaiting his visit.

Juanita, Esther, and I finished the clinic, had our tea, sat on a log, and looked out over a series of beautiful, hazy valleys and mountains that stretched into the mysterious uncharted distance. We waited and waited for my husband. At last Bill finished, and we were on our way.

Since we had supplies to leave at another school, we stopped there on our return trip. Again my nursing colleagues and I waited and waited and waited. Finally I went to see where Bill was. I found him putting together a government-granted, wood cookstove for a domestic science class, which hadn't been assembled properly.

Later Bill decided I could drive to Helehele on my own. He gave me detailed instructions. "Turn off the road at a certain point. You'll have two streams to cross. The first one has a sandy bottom, and you must keep in the established tracks. The second stream is rocky, so don't tear the bottom out of the car. If you put the right wheel up over that large rock, you'll avoid the other stones that might do damage. Be careful not to drag bottom as you scramble up the bank. Shortly after the second stream, turn at the tree with a branch that looks like a turning signal. Take the trail that leads up the mountain. After a certain curve you will find a muddy area. Be prepared to decide immediately after the curve whether to drive straight through the mud or if you need to curve up on the bank, while not losing your speed. The last bit is very steep and over shale rocks. Just be careful!"

A real excursion for a jeep enthusiast!

The treacherous road to Helehele

I visited this clinic for months. Many African moons had come and gone. Over time the road deteriorated to such an extent that I refused to drive. Dr. Howard Hamlin, who was then the hospital chief at Manzini, said, "I want to see this road that you refuse to drive." He possessed a long, lovely American vehicle.

"I don't think you ought to try to take your nice big car up the mountain," Bill warned him.

Dr. Hamlin said he wanted to try anyway. He did, but quickly he gave up, changed his mind, and rode with us.

At the community meeting in Helehele, the people asked, "At what point of the road do you find it difficult to drive? If we build you a clinic at

Mshingishingini school, which is closer to the road, will you go there?"

"Certainly." I thought little more about my promise.

Sometime later a committee reported that my clinic was ready at Mshingishingini. We set a date. They had built a small, one-room clinic of poles, mud, and thatch—complete with a little veranda and a vase of flowers on it. We had to transport all medicines, water, and equipment from Piggs Peak. The school children from Helehele had carried on their heads the steel medicine cupboard and the patient's bench several miles down to the new clinic. At our first visit we treated 60 patients.

Medical assistance was a practical tool to show God's love. It was also an ongoing opportunity to teach health principles. When we had access to a huge supply of UNICEF powdered milk, we distributed this to the clinics. Once a patient asked, "What kind of a cow gives milk like this?"

Proud of my rural background, I told her, "A dry cow."

On one visit to Mshingishingini clinic, a patient with pneumonia came in. She was most interesting as she wore all the paraphernalia of a witch doctor— many bracelets on her arms and around her neck amulets, animal bladders, and red "dread naughts" waxed with floor polish. I was happy that her illness could be treated with an antibiotic. Her major illness, however, could not be treated with medicine. With my helper, a woman of the Bible, we asked her, "Would you like to be rid of the demons?"

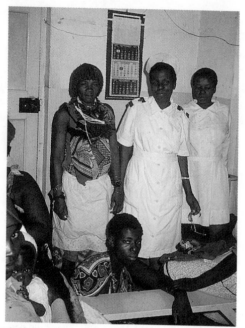
Witch doctor with nurses at Nazarene clinic

With a voice of scorn and disbelief, she replied, "You obviously are a white person, or you wouldn't ask me such a foolish question. Everything I have— my bracelets, charms, the clothing I have on, every- thing I own—belongs to the demons. I live alone in the forest. They still demand more. Even now they are laughing at you."

As I looked into her eyes, a chill went up my spine. I felt that I was truly looking into the eyes of the demons. I remembered Uncle Jenkins words, "When you see it, you won't need a label."

5

Trauma and Tragedy

I was crying so hard when I boarded the plane the flight attendant asked if Bill and I were recently married. We had just ended our second furlough and faced the painful, heart-wrenching time of leaving Beverly in the United States while we returned to Swaziland.

Upon our arrival at Endzingeni, we went to Juanita Gardner's house down by the tabernacle for lunch. The annual women's meeting was in progress. Soon we heard quite a ruckus and looked out a window. The whole batch of women were marching, singing, and swaying, over to Juanita's house. They were coming to give us a warm welcome. Surrounding us with true Swazi affection, everyone wanted to shake our hands. One woman decided to kiss my feet, much to my chagrin. It was certainly a temporary soothing balm to my distressed heart.

A revival tide swept the meetings in progress. I remembered seeing people "run the aisles" back in the States, but I had never seen anyone "dance the aisles." The Holy Spirit was so in evidence we staid missionaries observed that anyone who couldn't dance hit the altar. The spirit of revival continued for

Welcoming the Moons back to Endzingeni after furlough

some time, spreading next door in the girls' hostel and then out to the surrounding churches.

At Endzingeni we received a new assignment. Since Arthur and Dorothy Evans were due to furlough, a replacement was needed. Bill's job was to be adviser to the zone chairman, Rev. Richard Gininda. This position involved preparing the district to become a regular district, fully self-supporting and self-governing. Instead of dealing with the schools and their problems, now Bill's task was to help the local churches. He was also the head of station with all the responsibility that entailed. I would be the clinic "sister" when Juanita Gardner left for her home assignment. Thankfully, the Endzingeni clinic was not as busy as the one at Piggs Peak.

We enrolled Mike in a boarding high school in

White River, South Africa. The school was supposed to be bilingual, but it was strongly Afrikaans. For Mike it was a year of trauma. Americans were not the most loved people, and Mike had just begun to get his height. There never was enough food, he said. And to put it bluntly, he suffered at the hands of the upper-class students and the faculty. He tried to be tough and didn't tell us all until later. At his first visit home he had lost nine pounds.

✳ ✳ ✳

A new missionary family, Tom and Liz Bach and their children, Lee Ann and Bradley, were assigned to Endzingeni. Tom was a teacher in the high school and sponsored an outstation church in an outlying community on the weekends. Young in age and spirit, the Bachs were full of fun and enthusiasm.

In January 1970 little Lee Ann started school at Piggs Peak. Each day she met our neighbor Mollie Boyd, who operated the butchery in Piggs Peak, at the mission gate and rode with her to and from school. Often Tom and Liz picked up their daughter, Lee Ann, early on Friday, and sometimes the two children of Mrs. Boyd rode with them back to the mission to play until their mother came home.

In May of that year it was time for Mike's break from school in Nelspruit. (He transferred to another school after his difficult year at White River.) Missionaries Tom and Faye Riley were going to Nelspruit and offered to pick up our son and bring him to the Peak. We could meet Mike there.

As we stepped out on the veranda to go to Piggs

Peak, we saw a plume of smoke just before the forest of Peak Timbers, probably a mile from the mission. As we drove along, we wondered about this smoke, maybe something burning in the forest. No, it was on the road. When we came around a curve, we realized there had been an accident and an automobile was burning. We pulled up and stopped beside a tanker truck. Some Swazi women ran to our car and said, "There were some white people in the accident. We need help."

I leaned against the dirt bank and moaned, "O God, these things aren't supposed to happen to a missionary family. What's going on?"

A VW bug was in flames. Beside the road and carefully laid out on the bank were the bodies of Liz Bach and the two Boyd children. Liz had a dozen eggs still unbroken in a paper sack on her lap. Amazingly, there was no sign of burns on either of the three bodies. Even more amazing was the fact the Swazis, who normally do not like to touch a dead body, had taken them from the vehicle. I tried to give resuscitation to each of them and realized it was hopeless. I could find no vital signs.

As I was leaning over them, a tire from the burning car burst right behind me! I leaned against the dirt bank and moaned, "O God, these things aren't supposed to happen to a missionary family. What's going on?"

I turned and asked Bill, "Where's Tom?"

"Right here." Tom's charred body was still in the car. Evidently all had died instantly.

Bill spotted and retrieved Tom's open New Testament in the front seat. The verses from Romans 8:35-36 were underlined. One part of verse 35 stood out: "For thy sake we are killed all the day long" (KJV).

There was no sign of Lee Ann. Some Swazi women walking along the road had broken the rear window of the car and pulled unconscious Bradley out from the "dog box," the cubby hole behind the backseat, which was just big enough for a child to curl up and go to sleep. "We had to make him cry," the women said. "We pumped his arms like we do for a newborn baby." Then in their wisdom they said, "His eyes were too young to look on this scene, so we took him away into the forest."

The first passing motorist rushed Brad to the Peak hospital. Bill hurried to the nearest home with a phone and called for help. Then he dashed to a road junction to direct traffic around the area. We especially didn't want Mrs. Boyd to come upon the scene while on the way home until she had been warned.

An ambulance finally arrived and took the bodies to the government hospital at Piggs Peak. I went along to see after Brad. After a while, sitting numbly by his side, I felt a strong, vibrant arm across my shoulders—my son, Mike. What a comfort that was! Bill had driven our car to the Peak mission and brought Mike to the hospital.

Paul Riley and Kenneth Stark, doctors at the hospital in Manzini, on hearing the news by telephone left the emergency room at Manzini and rushed to the Peak. We heard that Paul's Mercedes "flew" the 60 miles up the hill without it ever touching the ground. They arrived at the hospital before any Peak Timbers or government doctors arrived from a short distance away. The missionary doctors with Bill identified the bodies of the Bachs, which were then transported to a funeral home in Manzini.

But where was Lee Ann? we wondered, so puzzled. Phone calls were made to see if she had decided to play with a school friend. We learned nothing.

The following day when the Bach's VW was moved, some men found the charred remains of what was believed a baby. It was Lee Ann.

"But how did this tragic accident happen?" everyone was asking. Since winter rains had not started, the dirt roads were chewed to a deep fine powder. The Bachs in their week-old Volkswagen were following a bus at a distance that evidently kicked up an incredible amount of dust. Both the VW and the oncoming tanker truck were in the middle of the road, and the drivers probably never saw each other.

The two doctors took Brad to the Nazarene hospital at Manzini. As he was quite restless, someone stayed with him continually. We drove Mike to the hospital where he found Brad's room and crawled into bed with him. One of the missionaries heard Mike say, "It's me, Brad. I'll be here when you wake up."

Brad relaxed and said, "OK, Mike." And the critically injured boy promptly went to sleep.

Community and missionary family support all went into action. We operated on some inner automatic pilot. This was a land without a "friendly undertaker." The Boyd children were taken to a funeral home in Nelspruit and buried on the family farm, next to their father who had died only a few months previously.

Saturday was payday, and the Peak village was usually jumping and boisterous with everyone coming to shop. On the Saturday following the accident, the merchants told us that it was eerie. People came in, bought their necessities, and left without a sound—almost like being on the big, bright African moon, it was so quiet.

The Bach's triple funeral was planned for Monday. The missionary family replaced their personal family. Mike and his friends were pallbearers for Lee Ann. Bill and the mission authorities planned the funeral. Three graves had to be dug. Swazi custom did not permit the graves to be open before the day of the funeral.

Monday morning Bill went to the burial site to supervise the preparation of the graves. He said he broke down and wept openly upon seeing a large number of Swazis at the cemetery with their shovels, ready to help dig the graves. Some he knew had walked 10 miles that morning to be there. Ropes for lowering the caskets had to be

The Bachs would be laid to rest beside pioneer Harmon Schmelzenbach and his children.

organized—just one of the things that had to be done but which people would never think of. The Bachs would be laid to rest beside pioneer Harmon Schmelzenbach and his children.

The tabernacle was packed with mourners. Bill along with many others gave tribute to the Bachs. Rev. Leonard Sibandze, the district superintendent, preached a powerful message from Luke 10:8-14. He charged the high school students and the whole community with the mandate that because these people, the Bachs, had come to help them and left not only their blood but their ashes in Swaziland, they should repent. If they did not, it would be worse for them than for Sodom and Gomorrah on the day of judgment.

It was staggering to think that any good thing could possibly have come from such a tragedy. However, it was a turning point in the attitude of the Swazis toward the missionaries. Swaziland was a newly independent country. Politicians with their influence had made known their disdain for white people, and this sentiment was creeping into the Christian community. Seemingly the people in general didn't realize how much they loved the missionaries, and there were times that we didn't sense much love toward us. Any doubts that we had, however, were erased with the people's outpouring of love and grief. It was a marvelous time of healing. By their death, the Bachs did more to establish and draw the church together during this time of its search for independence than they could have done in a lifetime.

Weevils and
Wedding Cakes

Ants invaded everything. Literally everything! A bit of moisture left overnight would attract one kind of ant, while another kind seemed to like sugar or starch content.

One day I made bread and left it to rise. I neglected to leave the bowl in a pan of water to form a moat from the invading ant army. When I returned, I found the dough literally covered with the pesky creatures. I tried to blow them off, but I didn't have enough "blow." I fetched Beverly's bicycle pump and blasted them away. Bill arrived in the kitchen and accused, "What are you trying to do? You think you can make the bread rise?"

A dear family from Omaha, Nebraska, sent us a huge supply of food storage containers from their local missionary chapter's Tupperware party. Any food not completely sealed in Tupperware was an open invitation for crawling visitors. Tupperware. What a blessing!

Another nuisance we encountered was weevils. Coming from dry Colorado, this was a new pest for me. In Swaziland weevils inhabited any kind of a flour product. I had to sift all flour through a silk screen that left a batch of little larvae wiggling on the net. Ugh! We had to check every box of spaghetti and look for telltale webs on the box. But after a while we learned to ignore most of them. Experience taught us three ways to deal with weevils in spaghetti: (1) Immerse the pasta in boiling water. With a slotted spoon lift the black blobs out as they come to the surface. (2) Hold the pasta in one hand and slowly let it down into the water. As the beasts come to the top, flip them off. (3) Always have a good supply of an herb on hand to add to the pasta. The weevils aren't even noticed.

Missionaries always had to expect the unexpected. People arrived unannounced on our doorstep with regularity. Unreliable phone service and irregular snail mail prevented making plans. Yet, we offered the customary cup of tea and a snack to every visitor.

One time two ladies from Mozambique were staying in our house as overnight guests. For breakfast I had cornflakes on the table. One woman had never seen this cereal and asked what it was. Bill explained that it was just corn crushed, cooked, rolled thin, and then toasted.

"My, my," she commented. "You did have to get up early this morning to fix our breakfast."

✻　✻　✻

My staid and dignified husband gave our house girl a small amount of a new and strange food to cook, which had arrived in a LINKS package. Popcorn. Bill told her to put oil in a frying pan over the fire and stir the popcorn continually until it was done. We left the room and listened. Suddenly, shrieks came from the kitchen. "Hau! Iya pupuma yonke." (Hey, it is all jumping out.) We found the girl, convulsed with laughter, still stirring the empty pan with popcorn everywhere.

We found the girl, convulsed with laughter, still stirring the empty pan with popcorn everywhere.

Missionaries encourage Christian weddings, and some Western traditions became entrenched in the proceedings. A wedding cake could never replace the traditional feast, but over time the cakes became taller and taller. The English royal icing could replace cement. Fruitcakes could be baked long in advance then coated with icing and held for the big day. My introduction to helping to cut the cake was a "royal" surprise. First I used a good silver knife with a lovely ribbon on the handle. It didn't work. The last effort was done in private with a hatchet.

Royal icing did have its good points, however. We attended a wedding down in the low veldt. At one point we had to leave the cars and cross a gully on foot, carrying the cake. One layer escaped the hands of the bearer and rolled down the hill while she watched it, screaming in dismay. No need to worry. The dirt was easily flicked off and decorations added upon arrival at the wedding site.

* * *

Word came of the death of Dr. David Hynd's wife. At that time I was the station hostess and called their daughter-in-law. "Phyllis, what would you like for us to do?"

"Would you please take care of cooking the cow for the feast?"

Cook a cow? I had visions of a Swazi arriving at my back door with a monstrous bovine on a leash ready to jump into my largest pot. After much gasping and stuttering, I agreed. Gratefully there were experienced and capable Swazi women that knew the exact procedure. With a large number of three-legged black iron pots, the cow was duly transformed into an adequate feast for the hundreds of people who arrived for the funeral. My function became a purely decorative one, ensuring appropriate care for the dignitaries and visitors.

Educating and
Evangelizing

Again we moved, first to Siteki, then later to Manzini. Bill was made the grantee for all the Nazarene schools in the country. At that time the church had 39 primary schools, 3 high schools, and the teacher's college. Bill's demanding position required that he serve on national boards that planned the future educational goals for the entire country. The Swaziland government paid the salaries of all the teachers and often gave grants for buildings.

In the schools from grade one until the end of high school, a course called religious knowledge was taught. A more accurate name would be Bible knowledge. This course was taught during our time as missionaries not only in mission schools but in most schools in sub-Saharan Africa. People who did not know their Bible were considered "heathens," and no one wanted to be called a heathen.

This was a wide open door to teach and lead

youth to Christ. However, head knowledge of the Bible did not always translate into heart knowledge.

For a long time we tried to think of a profitable solution to this challenge. For many years the LINKS program of Nazarene Missions International (NMI) provided only $50 annually for our 40-plus schools. This was such a small amount that it got lost in the general supplies. Then a new policy was developed. We could ask for $50 for *each* named Nazarene mission school. Wow! How exciting!

We named them—Mshingishingini, Nhlanguya-vuka, Nhlangatana, Helehele, and on and on. That would mean $2,000 for the schools. Even so, what can a person do with just $50 for an entire school with several hundred students each? I believe God inspired us with the idea of hiring a school evangelist.

What a lady Juliet was! Dignified and soft-spoken, she possessed a "short line" to the Heavenly Father.

Who could it be? The most obvious choice was an outstanding preacher, Juliet Ndzimandze. But would she be willing? A woman of prayer, she was a warm, charming, and humble lady. Once she had been chosen to be one of the king's wives. She refused and left the country to escape his attention. Some time later, she returned to Swaziland but never married.

After much prayer and with fear and trembling, we went to Rev. Ndzimandze and asked if she would consider being the school evangelist. She was gracious and kind as she

**Rev. Juliet Ndzimandze preaching
at a school in Swaziland**

said, "Why did it take you so long? God spoke to me long ago about this."

What a lady Juliet was! Dignified and soft-spoken, she possessed a "short line" to the Heavenly Father. She demanded respect wherever she went. (Her story is told in the book *Daughter of Africa*.)*

Rev. Ndzimandze's plan was to spend four days at a school. She would have at least two daily evangelistic sessions with the children. First she preached to the young ones. After they left, she then had a service with the older students. Time was made for

---

Daughter of Africa by Chuck Gailey. An NMI book for 1998-99. Nazarene Publishing House.

fellowshipping, counseling, and praying with the teachers.

This is an example of Juliet Ndzimandze's appeal after her presentation of the gospel message:

"All right, children. I'm going to dismiss you. You have a long way to walk home, and your mothers are waiting for you to carry wood and water. I want all of you to leave the room. However, I'll be here waiting. If one of you is really serious and wants to accept Christ into your heart, come back and we will pray." The children would stream out and then come right back in to their seats.

"You have returned," the evangelist would say. "Thank you. Now just what is it that you want Jesus to do for you?" She asked several individually. Instruction was given on how to kneel, pray, confess, and accept Christ.

After a time of prayer, while she walked through the rows of chairs and touched each curly head, they would be seated again. "Now who would like to tell us what Christ has done for you?" As the children stood to testify, she listened intently. If a child just repeated what the last one said, the evangelist said, "No, I want to know what Christ did for *you*." If she wasn't satisfied with the answer, she would say to the child, "Sit over there. We will talk some more."

Juliet Ndzimandze faithfully kept lists of those who accepted Christ. On the closing Sunday she would have a regular service at the local church when she would call all the teachers to the front and present them with the lists, charging them with the

**High school students working through
the *Basic Bible Studies***

responsibility to disciple the new believers. "You are
their leaders," she said with authority. "The children
will follow you wherever you go."

One teacher told me, "Rev. Ndzimandze impressed me so much that I felt that the list would
meet me in heaven, and I would be asked to give ac-
count of each of the children."

The teachers came to the Evangelism Committee
with the request to have materials to help all these
children learn what it was to be a real Christian. Chic
Shaver's *Basic Bible Studies* from Nazarene Publishing
House were a great help. These important lessons for
growing Christians were translated into SiSwati for the
seventh and eighth grades. Teachers faithfully used
them in the high school. The Evangelism Committee

prepared a simpler edition for the younger children. Eventually mission personnel wrote 13 lessons of stories or object lessons for the teachers to use, and a Bible study served as homework.

Missionaries John and Sandy Estey traveled to most of the schools ahead of the scheduled revival and worked with the staff, teaching them how to use the lessons and giving them counsel as well. The teachers used hundreds upon hundreds of these Bible studies.

Communists and Cornmeal

Revolution engulfed Mozambique. The general unrest and resentment against the Portuguese were fueled and funded by the Communist regime. A guerrilla-type warfare raged for years. This ferment finally culminated in the complete defeat of the Portuguese government in 1975. Portuguese fled the country. Missionaries Armand Doll and Hugh Friberg were imprisoned, then later released. While no missionary met serious harm, none remained in Mozambique.

The old Tavane mission station became a military camp. Our Bible school there was destroyed; the students scattered. The avowed goal of the rebels was to stamp out the church. Congregations were separated and dispersed to distant corners of the country. A number of believers were killed outright. It was a time of terror and suffering for the country.

Living in bordering Swaziland, we heard reports that made our hearts bleed. We had occasional opportunity to connect with the people from Mozambique. One was an airline employee. Meeting over coffee, we asked, "What about the church now that the missionaries are all gone?"

"Minha Senora, why would you ask such a question? We were not taught to worship missionaries. We were taught to worship God." Bill and I were thrilled and humbled.

Years passed while hundreds of African moons shone on the troubled land. The Mozambique mission director, Frank Howie, who lived in Johannesburg at that time, had contact through the Mozambique miners in the Joburg area. Though the war continued, tensions eased a little. In 1981 Frank made a few tentative trips into the country. Excited and blessed with the spirit he found there, it was heartbreaking to see the condition of the people and the country. But the faith of the Christians was strong. They were attempting to begin a few Bible school classes with the ministers and others who desired to preach. Frank encouraged them as best he could and provided some study material that was scarce.

In 1984 we received another phone call. Frank and his wife, Heather, were due for a home assignment. Would Bill relieve him and serve as mission director for Mozambique as well as continue being mission director of the education work in Swaziland? Bill didn't even ask me. His immediate answer was "yes."

What about our Portuguese language after 25 years of neglect? we wondered. Though excited, we had so many questions.

That year we made a journey back to Mozambique. Meeting with the leaders of the five districts, we asked them to tell us frankly what they felt was their most urgent need.

As an outside observer, my nursing senses went into play. I noted the signs of vitamin and protein deficiencies. I thought of the tightened belts that poorly disguised the effects of years of living on their ration of 1,200 calories daily, if they could find it. Their monthly food allotment was five kilograms of starch (rice, cornmeal, flour, or pasta), one half liter of oil, one half

The Communist regime had destroyed all Bibles and religious literature that they could find.

kilogram of sugar and tea, and one half bar of soap. Surely food and clothing would be their first request. "What is your greatest need?" we asked.

"Vafundisi (Missionaries), what we need most of all is something Christian to read in our language!" The Communist regime had destroyed all Bibles and religious literature that they could find. Some had kept what little they had hidden, even buried in the sand.

One day the government officials came to our district superintendents and said, "If we return some of your property, can you take the youth and do something with them?" This challenge was thrown to Bill.

What could we possibly do? After prayer and consultation, the leaders were invited to Swaziland for a workshop. Materials were found and translated

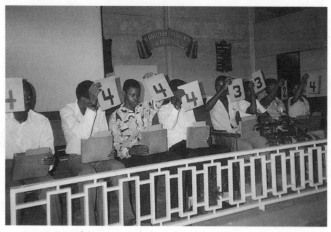
Mozambican youth involved in Bible quizzing

for Bible quizzing. Each district, supplied with all the necessary materials, made a set of quiz boxes. This program was far more successful than we could imagine.

One day Bill casually asked the Mozambican church leaders, "Would a youth camp be possible?" Words once spoken could not be retrieved.

"We're going to have a youth camp," came the announcement. "This generation has never had one." The word spread like wild fire.

But where could it be held? we wondered. After considering several alternatives, we decided to conduct it at Maputo Central Church. Boys could sleep on the floor, and the girls could walk to another church a mile away.

"How many will come?"

"Oh, many, Vafundisi. Many."

"But how many is *many?*"

"Many will come," the response came, accompanied by a chuckle.

"What about food?"

"We don't have any food."

We had decided on a maximum limit of 600 youth, ages 16–25. No more! And this youth camp would run from Thursday through Sunday.

We made an emergency call to Compassionate Ministries in Kansas City. We were allocated $2,500. That would be $1.00 per day for four days for 600 youth, with a few dollars left over. Though grateful for that amount, we thought, *Maybe they can do that in the States where prices are cheap, but we also have*

**Rev. Fred Huff preaching at
the youth camp in Mozambique**

*to provide transportation for ourselves and two evange-
lists. Besides food, we need pots for cooking, basins for
washing dishes, soap, and buckets for carrying water at
least two blocks from the nearest tap.*

This would certainly be a challenge—and an adventure. We purchased bags of beans, cornmeal,
peanut butter, and 600 loaves of bread in Swaziland
and trucked them to Maputo.

Being the efficient organizers that we were, we
decided that we should arrive on Wednesday, one
day early, to see that all was in order. With us would
be the two preachers, Fred Huff and Grace Masilela,
a converted witch doctor who was then our current
school evangelist.

Since no public transport was available and the
road still not safe, we called Solomon Macia, the Maputo District superintendent, on Monday to tell him
our arrival time and to have someone meet us at the
airport.

Rev. Macia picked us up and took us to the
same guest house in which we had stayed when we
had first arrived in Africa over 25 years before. The
place looked familiar, just many years older—with
no repairs. Several church leaders greeted us and offered us cups of tea. About 1:00 P.M. after a few
minutes of chatting, Solomon Macia began fidgeting
and finally blurted out, "Mufundisi, they are waiting."

"Who is waiting?"

"We heard you were coming a day early, and we
didn't want to waste your time. Some have already
arrived."

"But we are only prepared for four days," Bill started to protest. We had struggled to prepare some classes using Portuguese, and we weren't confident we could stretch the classes another day.

"What about additional food?" we questioned. "And all those extra meals? It will mean at least 1,000 extra meals!"

"Mufundisi, haven't you ever heard of the loaves and fishes?"

"God has given me a message," Grace said. "I'm ready!"

God did stretch our "loaves and fishes"—or should I say beans and cornmeal.

We went to the church selected for the campsite. Much to our surprise about 500 had already gathered. Later a final count revealed that almost 1,000 registered, when we wanted to max out at 600. And yes, the food did last. God did stretch our "loaves and fishes"—or should I say beans and cornmeal.

What an outpouring of blessing this camp was, not only for those who attended but to us as well. We saw young people bumping into each other as they ran to the altar. "Is this for real?" I asked a colleague.

"Do you remember where you are?" came the reply. "These young people face all kinds of challenges for becoming Christians. They don't accept this lightly. Following Christ here gives no guarantee of an easy life, or even daily bread."

In the food shipment we had purchased a car-

**District superintendents accepting the
gift of grape Kool-Aid**

ton of mixed Kool-Aid as a treat. The five district superintendents spotted it immediately. "May we have
permission to take the packets of grape Kool-Aid?"
they asked, their voices filled with excitement.
"We'll divide it among our pastors. With the Kool-
Aid we can have proper Communion with our people at home."

Blockades and Bulletproof Bubbles

"Bill, a lady at that last church asked if I was ever afraid."

My husband chuckled. "I have a snapshot memory of you on top of a steel drum in the storeroom, screaming your head off because you had disturbed a rat's nest. By the way, how did you get on top of that drum? Or who was it that disappeared under the bed covers when an innocent little bat came down the chimney for a visit?"

I laughed as Bill brought back those memories, pretending my innocence. "Remember that unnerving incident at the Peak when those angry men invaded the mission?"

Bill nodded his agreement as he continued driving down the interstate. We were traveling to the next church on our deputation schedule. On our numerous travels across America and Canada, Bill and I had lots of time to reminisce and share our thoughts and feelings. These times of remembering were special moments to both of us.

The particular event I was recalling happened during the time of preindependence unrest in Swaziland. About 35 men from the hostel at Endzingeni marched all the way to Piggs Peak. Riots and strikes were everywhere. Those men were demanding and belligerent, yet Bill was so calm and dignified. After talking with the angry fellows, Bill told them that he would meet them back at Endzingeni the next day and confer with them and their leaders.

"Bill, I was so scared, but I'll never forget what you said to me, 'I'm going to bed and get some sleep. We have no phone. If these men want to harm us, there's nothing we can do, God is in control.'"

"That is one of those unforgettable moments for sure," Bill commented.

"Remember that man who came at me with a knobkerrie?" I asked.

"Sure do."

"The Lord certainly helped me that day."

My mind took me back to that Sunday I made a casual visit to the clinic. Hearing a commotion, I went to investigate. I learned that it was over one of our new mothers who had a severe pelvic infection. And since she still had a fever, we were treating her with an antibiotic. That particular day her husband had come for her, as it was time to be plowing the fields. Drunk and combative, he commanded her to climb in the back of his truck. With his knobkerrie (a Swazi club) he gave her a couple of whacks across her back. The woman ran behind me for protection. He then turned his ire on me, raising his club and cursing. It was if a bulletproof bubble had surrounded me. No, I wasn't being brave. I just stood my ground secure in the knowledge that he couldn't touch me.

"That was how I felt when we lived at Endzingeni," Bill responded, "when I was in bed with a high fever. Remember?"

Bill had just dismissed one of his teachers for immorality, but her companion said he had taken her according to his custom. He came to our house one day, muscled his way in the bedroom, and threatened to kill my husband.

A young woman caught my attention who crawled up the steps, making sounds like an animal.

"How could I forget, Bill. That was so frightening. For all of us." I quickly added, "And do you remember the strange woman at Balekane?"

"Which strange woman? There seemed to be so many." Bill looked straight ahead, concentrating on the traffic in front of him.

"The one that crawled like an animal," I said, reminding my husband of this bizarre incident. I had had a heavy day in the clinic, seeing numerous patients. A young woman caught my attention who crawled up the steps, making sounds like an animal. Whenever she could get my eye, she would call out to me—no words, just sounds of pleading for help. A young student witch doctor had accompanied her. The sick girl had been given medicine of some kind to drive out her illness. Somehow, something went wrong, so they brought her to the white woman for an injection.

I tried to tell her that I would have to take her to the hospital in Manzini and have the doctors there treat her. I also explained that the medicine we gave her and the witch doctor medicine would not mix. Since the girl was a minor, she needed permission for me to take her to the hospital. Her sister who was with her said she would go and try to obtain permission.

At dusk I was loading up all the empty bottles and empty paraffin (kerosene) tins for the fridge. I looked up and here came an apparition—that reminded me of the devil himself—riding on a bicycle. He had all the paraphernalia of his trade: skins, bladders, tails of the wildebeest, hair done up in the fashion of his trade. He started screaming curses and epithets at me from the minute he entered the grounds of the clinic. I stood as if I didn't understand a word he was saying, and fortunately I didn't understand it all. And as I stood staring at him, I was aware of that bubble around me."

"That bubble was around us many times," Bill interjected. "Like the time we were at an outstation checking on a building project in the community and zillions of angry men confronted us."

"That is one of those indelible moments," I commented. "We certainly felt the bubble of God's protection that day."

Bill continued the story, refreshing our memories. It happened during all the disturbances before elections and independence. Hundreds of men were leaving the mine because they were on strike. They had chosen to gather at our mission station and decide what to do against all those "selfish white people" at the mine, as they referred to them.

Bill and I were caught in the middle of a throng of men carrying weapons of whatever kind they could find. In this vulnerable position, we had no defense, no idea what they might decide to do, no way to communicate with an authority. Nevertheless we did what we needed to do, and then left. The next day Bill went to the police and assured them that the mission had nothing to do with the strikes. They were astounded and said they were so afraid to go near the place that they only monitored the situation with binoculars from a distance across the valley.

"Ugh." I shuddered as Bill's words stirred up this ugly and scary time.

As we entered the outskirts of the next town, Bill continued talking. "Remember when we were working with the refugees in the Eastern Transvaal? And the man who had been 'necklaced'?"

"Ugh." I shuddered as Bill's words stirred up this ugly and scary time. He recounted the events of that day. We were to go to a warehouse, buy supplies, and deliver them to the camps for which the Nazarene church was responsible. We had heard accounts of trouble. Reports and rumors were rampant. And we heard some poor victim not too far away had been "necklaced," that is, a gasoline-filled tire placed around his neck and set afire. But we decided to continue, as the Howies and the Riggs were with us. Our lorry and Land Rover were filled to the max with food stuffs.

Suddenly, on the ridge ahead of us we spotted a line of men across the road. Each had a heavy stone ready to throw at us. After a brief stop and conference with the other two couples, we realized we didn't know any other road by which to return to the mission or the camps. We had to proceed. Fortunately someone in each vehicle spoke the local tribal language. That way we were able to talk our way through. At one point some of the men tried opening the doors of the Land Rover and rocked it to see if they could turn it over. All of the occupants of the vehicles were "watching and praying"! After eight blockades we finally arrived at the mission.

When the Land Rover was returned to the Regional Office, the mission leaders found written in the dust on the side mirror, "OK."

"Did we have a guardian angel with us?" Bill asked rhetorically. "Were we in that bubble then?"

The stories went on and on and on. As many stories as there had been African moons. Often we faced difficult situations that were more dangerous than we realized at the time. However, a calm assurance didn't arise out of any kind of personal bravado. It was the promise, "My Presence will go with you" (Exod. 33:14, NIV).

Pronunciation Guide

The following information is provided to assist in the pronouncing unfamiliar words in this book. The suggested pronunciations, though not always precise, are close approximations of the way the terms are pronounced in English.

Acornhoek	AY-kohrn-hook
Afrikaans	AF-ree-kahnz
Alvaro Andrade	AL-vah-roh ahn-DRAHD
Bach	BAHK
Balekane	bah-luh-GAH-nay
bilharzia	bihl-HAHR-zee-uh
Endzingeni	end-zihn-GEH-nee
Germiston	JER-muhs-stuhn
Gininda	gee-NEEN-dzah
Helehele	HAY-lay-HAY-lay
Hoyo hoyo	HOH-yoh HOH-yoh
Komati	koh-MAH-tee
Kruger	KROO-ger
kwashiorkor	kwah-shee-OHR-kohr
Liga	LEE-guh
Limpopo	lihm-POH-poh
Lourenço Marques	loh-REHN-soh MARKS
Macia	mah-SEE-ah
Manzini	mahn-ZEE-nee
Maputo	mah-POO-too
Masilela	mah-see-LAY-lah
Mausse	mah-OO-say

Mbabane	mm-bah-BAH-nee
Minha Senora	MEEN-yuh sayn-YOH-rah
Moçamedes	moh-SAH-meh-dees
Mshingishingini	mm-SHIHNG-shihng-GEH-nee
mufundisi	moo-foon-DEE-see
Nazareno	nah-zah-RAY-noh
Ndzimandze	nn-dzih-MAHND-see
Nhlanguyavuka	nn-KLAHN-goo-yah-VOO-gah
Nhlangatana	nn-KLAHN-gah-TAH-nah
pensão	PEHN-sown
ponte	PAHNT
rondavel	rahn-DAH-vuhl
Senhor	SAYN-yohr
Shangaan	shahng-GAHN
Sibandze	see-BAHND-zee
Sibusiso	see-boo-SEE-soh
SiSwati	see-SWAH-tee
Siteki	see-TAY-gee
Tagus	TAY-guhs
Tavane	tah-VAHN-nee
vafundisi	vah-foon-DEE-see
Vasco de Gama	VAHS-koh day GAH-mah
Hau! Iya pupuma yonke	HOW EE-yah poo-POO-mah YOHN-kay